THUGHTFUL DIVERSITY

EMBRACING DIFFERENCES
FOR ORGANIZATIONAL SUCCESS

RODNEY C. AUSTIN

THOUGHTFUL DIVERSITY
EMBRACING DIFFERENCES FOR ORGANIZATIONAL SUCCESS

iUniverse books may be ordered through booksellers or by contacting:

iUniverse
1663 Liberty Drive
Bloomington, IN 47403
www.iuniverse.com
844-349-9409

Because of the dynamic nature of the Internet, any web addresses or links contained in this book may have changed since publication and may no longer be valid. The views expressed in this work are solely those of the author and do not necessarily reflect the views of the publisher, and the publisher hereby disclaims any responsibility for them.

Any people depicted in stock imagery provided by Getty Images are models, and such images are being used for illustrative purposes only.
Certain stock imagery © Getty Images.

ISBN: 978-1-6632-4394-2 (sc)
ISBN: 978-1-6632-4395-9 (e)

Library of Congress Control Number: 2022915155

Print information available on the last page.

iUniverse rev. date: 10/31/2022

ACKNOWLEDGEMENTS

My wife Suzanne for her endless inspiration, confidence, patience, and love.

My children, Raymond, Courtney, and Tai for giving me purpose, perspective and unwavering encouragement.

My advisors, Claudia Montanari, Jennifer Neilson, and Kendra Trahan for their invaluable support and suggestions.

My friend and brother Dave Rossi for believing in me and always being available as a sounding-board and counselor.

My Lord Jesus for giving me a vision and, hopefully, some wisdom that others may find useful.

CONTENTS

Resources

AUTHOR'S PERSPECTIVE

My professional career began forty years ago. Affirmative Action, a well-intended government program, had become accepted as something a business had to have in place to participate in government contracts and to appear socially conscious. Since that time, I have seen Affirmative Action progress from a strict focus on representation in the workforce to loftier ideals of diversity, equity, inclusion, belonging, and justice. My experience with what I will broadly call diversity has two facets, one personal and one professional, that are inextricably intertwined and form the basis of this book. Here is my story.

Personally, I was acutely aware of the vision, persistence, and literal sacrifice of so many who came before me to awaken the moral conscience of our nation and enact Affirmative Action legislation to open doors for minorities that were previously closed. Still, I was naïve and immature enough to believe that my high honors academic credentials, internship and work experience, varsity athletics, and demonstrated social and leadership skills were why I was courted and hired by a Fortune 500 company. I just *happened* to be Black.

So, which was it? Affirmative Action or merit-based on my accomplishments? Of course, it was both, but I will never be sure which was more significant. Was I the best candidate who just happened to be Black, or was I the best Black candidate to hire to meet a legal compliance goal? Thus, while I certainly benefitted from Affirmative Action (directly or indirectly), I would also be stigmatized by it.

My career progressed exceptionally well by any standard. I worked hard, delivered results, and was willing to learn and take risks. This led to an unusual career path for anyone—Black or white. I was afforded leadership positions in Human Resources, manufacturing operations, and product sales/service. I was well respected and valued as a contributor to many corporate-wide committees beyond my regular job. I was also usually the only Black person in the room. Flattered? Yes! Tokenized? Maybe. There was always an internal pressure to represent Black people favorably and, hopefully, open the door for others.

However, my highly unconventional career path had its detractors. There were questions (some directly, but most indirectly) about what qualified me for the job since I often didn't have the typical education or experience and hadn't served the time. How did I get to jump over others (whites) who seemed destined for the job? Would primarily white workforces respond to an outsider (young, Black, nontechnical background)? I successfully gained the trust and confidence of the employees in each situation—mainly through humility and listening—and with their help, met and often exceeded performance goals. But the passive/aggressive attitude about my abilities and qualifications for the opportunities I received still lingered for some, and caused me to doubt myself at times.

Professionally, I started my career as an HR generalist, and one of my first duties was working on Affirmative Action programs. I would diligently conduct local surveys, mine government data, and perform inane calculations to determine how many females or minorities needed to be hired into jobs in which they were considered "under-represented." (These calculations would often suggest that we needed to hire a percentage of a person. Never did I find that elusive half person!) The pressure to achieve the proposed representation in each job and avoid an internal or external audit led me to a tenacious pursuit of numbers. Filling the quota and checking the box was the goal. I believed that I was doing a great service for women and minorities. At that distant time, we were not talking about inclusion or creating an environment of belonging. The goal was to get representatives of targeted groups hired and hope they could navigate the organization on their own.

By the time I moved into senior and executive roles, I had gained a greater understanding of diversity, equity, and inclusion, and I was committed to being a better advocate. I brought the diversity issue to the table and touted its potential benefits to the organization (beyond legal compliance). While none of my executive peers ever rejected the concept, few embraced it with real passion or commitment. Diversity was acceptable as long as it was an HR process, and they did not have to expend time or energy on it. I encountered this attitude toward diversity throughout my career and, frankly, did not have much success in changing it. I had some diversity wins—a few glimpses of excellence—but never the sustained, culture-changing impact I wanted to see. Being the diversity champion in this type of environment was exhausting on many levels.

Since leaving the corporate world, I have started doing coaching and HR consulting. I have found (no surprise) that the general issue of diversity continues to be a challenge for former peers, colleagues, and prospective clients. In fact, the topic has become even more challenging and controversial in our current sociopolitical climate. I wanted to provide another approach—a guide to help them do diversity better.

After examining my own experience, discussing with colleagues, attending seminars, and reading numerous books and articles, I believe that the next level of diversity is the insistence on *diversity of thought* as a core element of organizational culture.

The pursuit of diversity of thought—or cognitive diversity—transcends the individual concepts of diversity, equity, inclusion, and belonging (DEIB). It embraces all of them as necessary to generate the myriad of experiences, ideas, and inputs needed to arrive at better answers and solutions, which will in turn produce superior results for the organization.

The concept of diversity of thought is not new. Making it a core organizational competency, an intention instead of a hope, is unique and transformative. When thought diversity is imperative, DEIB becomes less emotional and divisive and more logical and uniting.

Because you value different experiences, backgrounds, and perspectives, you will seek more *diverse* relationships. Because you desire a variety of thoughts, you will ensure *inclusive* systems and processes that encourage everyone to participate fully. Because you recognize the contributions of each person, you will provide for their needs with *equity*. Because you appreciate different thought processes, you will provide an environment where everyone feels safe to be their authentic selves with a sense of *belonging* to the larger organization.

The beauty of diversity of thought as an underpinning for your organization's success is that it is not a "winner take all" or "zero-sum" proposition—nor should it be! When a person or organization accepts that change and continuous improvement are vital to their success and longevity, and those improvements will come sooner and be more robust by considering perspectives that differ from theirs, they will be more receptive to nontraditional inputs. The fear of seeking or adding different people with different thoughts will be replaced by a curiosity and desire to learn and grow by these associations. There will also be the realization that diversity of thought means

- No group (or person) has to lose anything;
- No group (or person) needs to be replaced;
- No group (or person) must dominate;
- No group (or person) will be oppressed or left out; and
- No group (or person) will feel patronized.

Everyone is included because everyone has thoughts. Moreover, when one idea is added to other ideas, a synergistic effect is produced that generates a better outcome.

Curiously, a casual observation of our current United States society will find the influences of Native Americans, Europeans, Asians, African Americans, Central and South Americans, and many others are widely accepted and emulated. This gives credence to the notion that differences can be appreciated, enjoyed, and used to enrich everyone. Even so, we continue to use the markers of skin color, language, disability, age, sexual orientation, and gender to divide us.

I advocate moving beyond political correctness and legal compliance to a higher calling of intellectual and emotional safety, acceptance, and appreciation. Such progress will only be made when we move from the transactional gestures of diversity and inclusion (focusing on numbers and optics) to the transformational actions of equity and belonging (encouraging and valuing individual participation and input).

This little book is my contribution to making DEIB a reality in any organization. While the subject is complex, I have attempted to provide an actionable process to make it come alive. I trust that you and your organization will create a culture that embraces the possibilities that come from having diversity, equity, and inclusion, and that you will foster a sense of belonging for each team member. DEIB is the gateway to thoughtful diversity.

DEIB BASICS

Before we go further, let's define some basic terms and concepts.

DEIB DEFINITIONS

Diversity is "the condition of having or being composed of differing elements."[1] (Merriam-Webster)

Diversity is a fact.

Diversity is the objective, numerical, measurable, "pass or fail" test. Organizations either have diverse identities—gender, race, age, sexual identification, disability, religion, and veteran status—or they don't.

A more helpful definition in this context is the quality of being different or unique at the individual or group level.

Equity is "justice according to natural law or right … freedom from bias or favoritism."[2]

Equity is fairness.

Equity is being fair and impartial. It gives no one an advantage and supports those who need help.

Equity is giving people what they need to be successful. It should not be confused with equality, which is giving everyone the same thing.

---

[1] *Merriam-Webster*, s.v. "diversity (n.)," accessed February 3, 2021, https://www.merriam-webster.com/dictionary/diversity.

[2] *Merriam-Webster*, s.v. "equity (n.)," accessed February 3, 2021, https://www.merriam-webster.com/dictionary/equity.

A more helpful definition in this context is "the pledge of fair treatment, opportunity, and advancement while striving to identify and eliminate barriers." (Ernst & Young 2021)

Inclusion is "the act of including: the state of being included."[3]

Include is "to take in or comprise as a part of a whole or group"[4]

Inclusion is a choice.

Inclusion creates an environment that values and encourages all individuals to get involved as early as possible in their work environment's decision-making, planning, and execution phases.

A more helpful definition in this context is "bringing together and harnessing … diverse forces and resources, in a way that is beneficial." (Jordan 2011)

Belonging is the sense of being in a "close or intimate relationship."[5]

Belonging is a feeling.

Belonging is the feeling of security and support when a member of a particular group has a sense of acceptance, inclusion, and identity. It is when an individual can bring his or her authentic self to work.

Belonging is a fundamental human need that every human wants. It is the sense that you are cared about on an individual basis. It is an emotion that is a powerful motivator and the ultimate satisfier.

---

[3] *Merriam-Webster*, s.v. "inclusion (n.)," accessed February 3, 2021, https://www.merriam-webster.com/dictionary/inclusion.

[4] *Merriam-Webster*, s.v. "include (v.)," accessed February 18, 2021, https://www.merriam-webster.com/dictionary/include.

[5] *Merriam-Webster*, s.v. "belonging (n.)," accessed February 7, 2021, https://www.merriam-webster.com/dictionary/belonging.

Belonging is the desired result of diversity, equity, and inclusion initiatives and can be intentionally created and reinforced.

A more helpful definition in this context is the sense that one can be himself or herself and feel like part of a community.

TYPES OF DIVERSITY

This list is intended to increase sensitivity to the myriad of identities and associations an individual may have so that you can develop a culture that accepts people as they are or may become.

Gender: Generally, this speaks to the representation of men and women but may also include period of nonbinary genders. For example, 52 percent of the United States population are women.

Race/ethnicity: Race refers to distinctive biological or physical traits, while ethnicity more broadly covers cultural expression and identification. For example, 40 percent of the United States population is nonwhite.

Sexual Orientation/Identification: Sexual orientation is about who one is attracted to and desires to have a relationship with. Sexual identification reflects an individual's sexual self-concept.

Generational/Age: People from a wide range of different ages and representative of specific generations. For example, five different generations are now in the workplace for the first time in history.

Disability: This term recognizes individuals who have physical or mental challenges; 19 percent of the United States population has some form of disability.

Veteran: A veteran is a person who served in the active military, naval, or air service, and who was not discharged dishonorably; 8.6 percent of people in the United States are veterans.

Religious: This term signifies appreciation of significant differences in religious beliefs and practices. The Deptartment of Defense, for example, recognizes 221 religions.

Cognitive: This term focuses on different styles of thinking and problem-solving used to make associations or draw conclusions.

OBJECTIVE JUSTIFICATIONS FOR DEIB

Financial

- Racially and ethnically diverse companies outperform industry norms by 35 percent (Hunt, Layton, and Prince 2015).
- Gender diverse companies are 15 percent more likely to outperform industry norms (Hunt, Layton, and Prince 2015).
- Highly inclusive organizations generate 2.3 times more cash flow per employee, 1.4 times more revenue, and are 120 percent more capable of meeting financial targets (Gebreyes, n.d.).

Innovation

- Inclusive companies are "1.7 times more likely to be innovation leaders in their market" (Bersin 2019).
- Companies with more diverse management teams have 19 percent higher revenue due to innovation (Lorenzo, Voigt, Tsusaka, Krentz, and Abouzahr 2018).

Recruiting/Retention

- 76 percent of job seekers said a diverse workforce is important when considering job offers (Glassdoor 2021).
- "There are 76 million baby boomers, and 72.1% are white. The millennials are an even larger group with 87 million,

but much more diverse—only 56% are white" (Kurtz and Yellin, n.d.).

- "… more than half of people think their company should be doing more to increase diversity among its workforce". (Glassdoor 2021)

Productivity

- "Organizations with inclusive cultures are [three times] more likely to be high-performing" and six times more likely to be "innovative and agile" (Bourke and Dillon 2018, 85).
- Researchers found that when diverse teams made an organization decision, they outperformed individual decision-makers up to 87 percent of the time (Larson 2017).
- Organizations with above-average gender diversity outperform companies with below-average diversity by 46 percent (Moran 2017).

SELF-CHECK

Creating a workplace of diversity, equity, inclusion, and belonging (DEIB) is a journey that requires consistent attention from dedicated leaders. Here are some markers to help you determine where your organization is on this journey.

- We know why DEIB is vital to our organization and our organization.
- DEIB is part of our core values and organization strategy.
- Our management team reflects the diversity we aspire to achieve.
- We attract diverse candidates.
- We retain diverse candidates.
- Our managers are trained and equipped to lead a diverse workforce.
- We regularly ask employees what they think and how they feel.
- Employees have the opportunity to participate in DEIB training and initiatives.
- Our workplace practices and policies support DEIB.
- We have established DEIB success metrics.
- Communication processes exist to deliver information and receive feedback on DEIB.
- We are recognized for supporting diversity in our community.

If you are not satisfied with the current state of any of these markers, this book will help you determine how to make progress.

DEIB QUOTATIONS

"We need diversity of thought in the world to face the new challenges." —Tim Berners-Lee (Tim Berners-Lee Quotes. BrainyQuote.com, BrainyMedia Inc, 2022. https://www.brainyquote.com/quotes/ tim_bernerslee_179893, accessed August 26, 2022)

"Diversity is being invited to the party. Inclusion is being asked to dance." —Vernā Myers
(Vernā Myers, quoted in Cho 2016)

"Diversity of numbers is transactional; diversity of thought is transformational."
(Unknown)

"Strength lies in differences, not in similarities." —Stephen R. Covey (@StephenRCovey, March 7, 2012)

"Fairness does not mean everyone gets the same. Fairness means everyone gets what they need." —Rick Riordan
(Riordan 2011, page 67)

"Diversity: the art of thinking independently together." —Malcom Forbes (Malcolm Forbes Quotes. (n.d.). allauthor.com. Retrieved August 26, 2022, from allauthor.com Web site: https://allauthor.com/ quote/35292/)

"We need to give each other the space to grow, to be ourselves, to exercise our diversity. We need to give each other space so that we may both give and receive such beautiful things as ideas, openness, dignity, joy, healing, and inclusion." —Max de Pree
(de Pree 2004, 16–17)

"Gender equality is not only a women's issue—it's everyone's issue." —Nan Sa Aell Daung Paing (Nan Sa Aell Daung Paing, quoted in United Nations Office for the Coordination of Humanitarian Affairs 2019)

"True belonging doesn't require you to change who you are; it requires you to be who you are." —Brene Brown
(Brown 2017, page 40)

"Inclusion is not simply about physical proximity. It's also about advocating and intentionally planning for the success of everyone." (Unknown)

DEIB BENEFITS AND CHALLENGES

Benefits	**Challenges**
Better decisions	Slower Decisions
Improved employee engagement	Effective communication
Sensitivity to cultural differences	Cultural misunderstandings
Expanded recruiting pool	Developing/maintaining recruiting sources
Greater community exposure	Increased community expectations
Better reflect customers	More customer expectations
Knowledge sharing/mentoring	Generational trust and respect
Enhanced organization culture	Internal resistance to change
Powerful leadership statement	Sustaining leadership commitment

PREPARATION

Having covered the basics, we will now explore the steps needed to prepare yourself and your organization for the journey to thoughtful diversity through DEIB.

FIVE KEYS TO DEIB IMPLEMENTATION

Know your why: Develop the organizational imperative for pursuing DEIB so others can buy-in.

DEIB is a culture change: DEIB must be led and managed with intentionality to become embedded into the fabric of the organization.

Bring everyone along: Make sure DEIB initiatives are robust and inclusive so that no one feels left out or unable to contribute their thoughts and talents.

Don't overreach: Understand the organization's capacity for change, and don't be afraid to start small.

Listen: The keys to successful DEIB initiatives and implementations exist within your team.

KNOW YOUR "WHY"

"If your why is strong enough you will figure out how."
—Bill Walsh
(Bill Walsh. AZQuotes.com, Wind and Fly LTD, 2022. https://www.azquotes.com/quote/855126, accessed August 29, 2022.)

Like any journey, you need to start with the first step, and that is determining your "why."

If you can't articulate your "why" for yourself and your team, the chances of sustaining a successful DEIB process are poor. I suggest you *stop now*!

If you are doing DEIB because it is politically correct or someone said you must, it will be difficult to generate any interest or enthusiasm. Even if you honestly feel this is the right thing to do, you need to develop a more compelling message. Don't do it to check a box.

However you do it, understand, internalize, and embrace the importance of DEIB in accomplishing your organization's goals. Then clearly and regularly communicate it to your team so they can embrace it as well.

Tip: It might be helpful to ask yourself and your team these questions.

1. Why are diversity, equity, inclusion, and belonging good for your organization?
2. Why are diversity, equity, inclusion, and belonging good for your leadership team?
3. Why are diversity, equity, inclusion, and belonging good for your employees?
4. Why are diversity, equity, inclusion, and belonging good for your external stakeholders (customers, suppliers, investors)?
5. Why are diversity, equity, inclusion, and belonging good for your community?

6. What is the organization's case or justification for pursuing DEIB?

I was tasked with starting the US HR function for a large multi-national company. The biggest challenge was getting buy-in from my peers who ran the newly formed regional business units. Our European parent had acquired many small, regional companies with complete autonomy to run their business as they pleased, and it pleased them to have as little HR as possible. As a part of the US Executive team, I was able to get an afternoon to make the case for a more significant HR presence with more consistent HR practices. I did this by painting a picture of what HR could be for everyone, and then asking the team if they agreed why we shouldn't have it. We went methodically through each HR function, from recruiting to compensation and payroll to benefits, training and development, and so forth. I described what ideally could be and asked them why they shouldn't have it. They resisted until they couldn't defend not moving forward, often with encouragement from others on the team as they saw the light. By early evening, the team knew *why* HR needed to evolve into a new form to serve a new organization best, and I had permission and support to move forward.

DEIB IS A CULTURE CHANGE

"Culture is the widening of the mind and of the spirit."
—Jawaharlal Nehru
(The Quintessence of Nehru (1961) edited
by K. T. Narasimhachar, p. 120)

There is a parable about the sower and the seeds. As the sower casts seeds, some fall on hard, compacted ground and never have a chance to root, and birds quickly eat them. Some seeds fall on rocky ground and sprout shallow roots that soon fade away and die. Others fall among thorns, take root, and grow until the more established and aggressive weeds choke them out. Finally, some seeds fall on the prepared, fertile soil, blossom, and yield a substantial crop.

Similarly, you (the sower) must cultivate an organizational culture (the soil) that is receptive to a variety of people and ideas in the form of diversity, equity, and inclusion (the seeds). As these seeds germinate, they will sprout into a healthy plant of belonging (the blossom) that will generate an abundance of thoughts, approaches, and improvements (the yield) to differentiate and move your organization forward.

An insular, hardened culture will immediately reject diversity, equity, and inclusion (DE&I). A rocky culture may entertain DE&I with curiosity for a while but will soon lose interest. A thorny culture will tolerate DE&I until it feels threatened and undermines the effort. A prepared culture will embrace and support DE&I for the benefits of belonging and diversity of thought it brings to the organization. You must examine your culture and confront any aspects that will impede the adoption of DE&I.

Organization culture has been a hot topic for decades, and hundreds of books have been written. I will not attempt to add to that canon here. Instead, I emphasize that culture is the nurturer—or killer—of any cultural transformation, which is undoubtedly the case with diversity, equity, inclusion, and belonging.

One might summarize this modified parable as

$$\text{Culture} + (\text{Diversity} + \text{Equity} + \text{Inclusion})$$
$$= \text{Belonging} \rightarrow \text{Diversity of Thought}$$

Most CEOs and leaders recognize the importance culture has on the success or failure of an organization. Culture can even be a competitive advantage when aligned with organizational goals. It has been said that culture eats strategy for breakfast. Simply adding a DEIB program or project to your strategy plank is likely to be rejected by the culture if you aren't clear and intentional in working to create the desired new culture.

DEIB must be a movement, a concerted effort to ingrain new behaviors, beliefs, and attitudes into the organization's value system. Intentionality is key. Managerial courage is required. Unwavering support is demanded.

Tip: Implement a change management process to prepare and support the organization through the transition to new behaviors, attitudes, and expectations. Like any other culture change DEIB, must

1. be modeled and led by top leaders;
2. be clearly communicated;
3. be given necessary resources (time, talent, treasure);
4. be supported by training;
5. be reinforced by recognition; and
6. be driven by data.

BRING EVERYONE ALONG

"Don't cause exclusion while trying to create inclusion."
—Rodney C. Austin

For diversity, equity, inclusion, and belonging to gain traction and achieve the desired impact, make sure everyone is involved. This includes white males.

While the focus of DEIB will (and should) be on historically disenfranchised groups, white males need to feel part of the process and not victims of it. Their support—or lack of support—correlates highly to the success and staying power of your DEIB movement.

Bring white males along by demonstrating that diversifying the workforce increases the firm's long-term viability (diversity of thought leads to richer inputs and better decisions) and, thereby, enhances their jobs and careers. It means more inclusive systems and processes do not exclude them, and they will benefit from the changes as much as every other group.

The focus is on *adding* to the mix and creating a broader spectrum of thoughts and ideas. The whole concept is synergy, where elements of different views and approaches to a problem yield a far better solution than any individual input. In this way, every idea is desired, solicited, and considered so that everyone has the same chance to participate, collaborate, contribute, and enjoy the success of the team's accomplishments.

Everybody gets to play, learn, grow, and benefit from meaningful interactions with everyone else—and the team wins.

Tip: Look for opportunities to create diverse working groups or pairings, in safe environments, focused on achieving a specific result. This will reinforce the goal of diversity of thought and allow team members to become more comfortable working with those who have different experiences and perspectives.

I had a valuable mentoring experience early in my career. As a young manager, I was assigned a mentor who was the Chief

Information Officer. He was older, white, Ivy League-educated, and obviously, had been very successful. Our backgrounds were practically inverse. However, we developed a great admiration for each other and learned a great deal. He gave me insight into the challenges anyone would face in climbing the corporate ladder, such as being a servant leader. I was able to help him understand the attitudes of the new generation recruited into the company and my concerns about being one of the few Blacks in management. I believe our association helped us both become more open-minded.

DON'T OVERREACH

"Less is more."
—Robert Browning (Browning 1855)

Recognizing the importance of DEIB to your organization is essential. You may be impressed by the success (real or imagined) that some companies purport and for which they are recognized. While they may set benchmarks to strive for, don't try to catch up all at once. Their journey is not your journey.

It's okay to start your DEIB initiative with a modest, narrow focus if you lack the resources to do more. It is essential to have a goal and a plan, commit to it, and get started.

If a particular DEIB area is troublesome, or, conversely, an area where you can have a quick win, that may be the best place to begin. Set your organization up for success by focusing on something achievable and getting a small win.

A small win creates excitement. Accumulated small wins build momentum. Momentum creates progress. Progress is visible and gives credibility to future goals and actions.

Small Wins > Momentum > Progress > Credibility
= Future Goals and Actions

It is better to have small successes than to overcommit and under-deliver and lose credibility.

Communicate the goal and break it into smaller pieces so everyone can understand it and support it. Be transparent about progress and setbacks and keep pushing forward.

Tip: DEIB should have a vision, strategy, tactics, goals, and a timeline like all vital initiatives. When this plan is formulated and overlayed on top of the other organizational business plans, you will be able to determine what is reasonable to accomplish given competing needs for resources (time, talent, and treasure). Management and employees will take DEIB seriously when they know a plan has been thoughtfully developed and vetted. A goal without a plan is a dream and will not be credible or sustainable.

In one company, we desired to have more female and minority engineers and agreed to expand our college recruiting efforts. We reached out to several schools and spread our budget and talent among them. Because our efforts were diluted, we did not attain the visibility and impact we needed to get the recruits we wanted. We also competed against larger, well-known companies that hired many more engineers each year. We then decided to partner with one school and concentrate our resources there. In addition to some specific project funding, we provided internships, plant tours, and guest speakers. We became a known and valued entity among that school's students and faculty. As our profile increased, we became a desired employer for their engineering students and were able to attract the diverse recruits we sought. By concentrating our resources on *one* school, we got better results.

LISTEN

"Seek first to understand, then be understood."
—Stephen R. Covey
(Covey 1989, 237)

Successful leaders recognize that the importance of communication is not just in delivering messages but also in soliciting and receiving feedback.

Listening is a voluntary act of intentionally focusing on the verbal and nonverbal reactions and feedback from others. It should not be confused with hearing, which happens involuntarily as a natural response to sound and noise. Listening requires curiosity, vulnerability, and acknowledgment (if not acceptance) of other viewpoints.

Listening is free. However, it does require time, concentration, sincerity, and intentionality.

Listening fosters participation, which leads to engagement. You will be impressed with the ideas and insights your team will provide to accelerate your DEIB culture change.

Listening is an ongoing activity, not a one-and-done event. Pay attention to what the team is saying and observe how they are acting (or reacting) to reinforce your message or modify your course if needed.

Tip: Seek input from your team members or associates.

1. Give them a safe forum to provide feedback and suggestions.
2. Probe (nonjudgmentally) for more or clarifying information.
3. Take some time to consider the feedback and how it can be used.
4. Provide sincere and timely responses. Associates can accept "no" as an answer if they feel heard and a thoughtful reason is provided.

As a production plant manager, I faced the challenge of absorbing a new product line that would necessitate increasing our productivity (output) by a third without adding personnel. The management team discussed the situation and developed plans that might achieve the goal, but we held them until we could present the challenge to the workforce (which we did in two large all-hands meetings). We gave them all the information available and noted that we had this opportunity because senior management had confidence in them. I also pointed out that accomplishing this would give the plant greater importance to the business, encourage future capital investments, and provide more stability for the workforce. They suggested things that we as managers were fearful of trying to implement due to concerns of a rebellion. We could—at their suggestion—gain half a shift of production by staggering employee time off for breaks, lunches, and shift changes. Engaging and listening to the workforce allowed us to kill the sacred cow of downtime with consent instead of opposition. There were other ideas—a diversity of thoughts, some implemented and some rejected—but we reached the goal much easier and quicker because we listened.

IMPLEMENTATION

Now that you've prepared, it's time to launch your DEIB plan. Following these implementation stages will help you succeed.

DEIB Implementation Flow Chart

MANAGEMENT PREPARED

Supply:
1. Goal (Why?).
2. Training and Expectations.
3. Resources.

EMPLOYEES INVOLVED

Provide:
1. Information (Why?).
2. Training and Expectations.
3. Feedback Loop.

PEOPLE SYSTEMS ASSESSED

Look for:
1. Bias / Inequity.
2. Meeting employee needs.
3. Updates and Fixes.

LEADERSHIP ALIGNED

Determine:
1. "Why" this is important.
2. Strategic Plan.
3. Accountability.

PROCESS SUSTAINED

Ensure:
1. Embed in Culture.
2. Reinforce Behaviors.
3. Adjust Plans as needed.

RESULTS MEASURED

Establish:
1. Goals.
2. Communication Cadence.
3. Measurement Systems.

Achieving a culture of diversity of thought will be accelerated with the successful implementation of diversity, equity, inclusion, and belonging initiatives. In words and actions, commit to DEIB goals and plans to set expectations and model desired behaviors.

The DEIB Implementation Flow Chart is explained in the following pages. The six implementation stages should be scaled to the organization's size but need to be considered and addressed in some form.

STAGE 1: LEADERSHIP ALIGNED

The organization will not embrace diversity, equity, inclusion, and belonging until the executive leaders make it a priority, and make it safe to do by modeling, encouraging, and recognizing the desired behaviors at all levels of the organization. The executive leadership team needs to have a shared understanding, commitment, and unity to DEIB. To align your leadership team:

1. Start with an executive meeting (or meetings) dedicated to developing the organization's "why" for pursuing diversity of thought and DEIB. All participants must share their thoughts, hopes, and concerns for DEIB to flesh out the potential pain points and root causes for resistance or failure. The Five Whys technique is an excellent way to discover why DEIB is essential to your organization.

    Using a trained and trusted meeting facilitator (internal or external) can also help manage emotions and keep the agenda on track. The goal is to emerge with a compelling and unified DEIB message that fosters buy-in and participation from the organization at large to produce thought diversity.

2. Develop the vision, mission, strategy, and goals for DEIB that support the organization's broader vision. The strategic plan needs input from the entire executive team for a shared sense of ownership and responsibility.

3. Establish accountability among the leadership team. While all leaders must be constant messengers and supporters of the agreed-upon DEIB strategy, one should be designated as

the visible go-to leader to drive the DEIB plans, activities, and resources, and serve as the liaison between the executive team and supporting DEIB groups.

Consider some visible actions to demonstrate leadership commitment to DEIB such as these.

- Establish an internal diversity council. A diversity council serves as an internal advisory board to the CEO and executive team. Put high-potential employees on your council to increase the visibility and importance of the DEIB initiative.
- Provide resources like

  o Time (make it okay to work on DEIB issues);
  o Talent (internal and external resources); and
  o Treasure (provide budgets for training, recognition, and other events).

- Set DEIB expectations and goals with accountability and measures. They may be a little "soft" to start, but they will become more firm and clear as your DEIB journey progresses.
- Report on DEIB regularly in a similar fashion to financial, customer, safety, or quality reports. Having tracked and reported goals will give DEIB credibility as an essential business function.
- Join external diversity and inclusion organizations as a visible public sign of your commitment to DEIB. This can be an excellent opportunity to form support networks and increase your knowledge of best practices in this area. CEO Action and Catalyst are national groups to consider.
- Listen. Provide methods for employee feedback. Be vulnerable, not defensive. This is the key to unlocking thought sharing.

"You cannot conquer what you are not committed to."
—T. D. Jakes
(Jakes 2016)

STAGE 2: MANAGEMENT PREPARED

Managers and supervisors have significant roles in fostering a culture that values diverse thinking and promotes DEIB since they are the face of the organization to employees every day. Their daily interactions will show whether the organization supports a diverse, equitable, and inclusive culture. Allow managers and supervisors to become comfortable in supporting the DEIB initiative by doing the following.

1. Informing managers and supervisors of the DEIB mission, vision, and strategy. Allow them to ask questions and express concerns. They need to understand the goal—the reasons DEIB is critical to the organization and the employees—if they are to be ambassadors for the cause.

2. Investing in DEIB-related training to raise management awareness, establish expectations, and provide tools such as:

    - Unconscious bias training;
    - Team dynamics training;
    - Creating an inclusive workplace;
    - Diversity awareness, to help people understand the benefits of working with a diverse organization;
    - Diversity management, to equip executives to manage diverse teams;
    - Professional development, to ensure that women, LGBTQ+, and ethnically diverse employees are included to build skills necessary for advancement; and
    - Listening skills, to encourage others to share thoughts.

3. Ensuring managers and supervisors understand the path forward and where to get resources and support. Perhaps there is a DEIB committee or champion, or maybe it is Human Resources or their manager. Don't leave managers on an island; it will frustrate them and kill the process in their areas.

As your DEIB process matures, individual manager/supervisor performance concerning DEIB initiatives can be evaluated as part of the annual performance management system. [See Resource IV for sample goals.]

"You must embrace change before change erases you."
—Rob Liano
(https://robliano.wordpress.com/2013/10/23/
change-is-good-you-go-first/)

STAGE 3: EMPLOYEES INVOLVED

Employees need to feel that DEIB is not being done *to* them, but being done *with* them and *for* them. Make them aware of leadership's commitment to DEIB through presentations at team meetings, internal memos, newsletters, year-end reviews, and other communication vehicles. Keep employees knowledgeable and involved by

1. Being transparent. Employees need to know the organization's objectives for pursuing DEIB. They also need to understand how it affects them or answers the WIIFM question (what's in it for me). Transparency is crucial to building trust and engagement in the DEIB efforts;[See Resource II for sample announcements].

2. Providing DEIB awareness training to help employees appreciate new perspectives and gain sensitivity to the shared and unique journeys they and their coworkers experience. However, conducting awareness training is a beginning and not a destination. Continuous monitoring of conflicts and pain points will allow more targeted training specific to the organization's needs; and

3. Developing a feedback loop that employees can trust as a safe place to express ideas and concerns. Regularly inform employees of short- and long-term DEIB aspirations, goals, progress, and even failures. This will promote trust, transparency, and engagement around DEIB initiatives.

Consider using some of these tools to engage your employees.

- Employee surveys to discover employee perceptions about DEIB, identify issues to address, and establish internal DEIB benchmarks to determine actions and measure progress. Share the results with employees to build trust for the initiative.
- Third-party review of organizational diversity and inclusion practices and employee perceptions to inform and recommend improvement plans and measures.
- Diversity awareness training to increase sensitivity to diversity issues and reinforce the organization's commitment to DEIB.
- Employee Resource Groups (ERGs) are support groups sharing specific traits and challenges (i.e., race, gender, sexual orientation, and so on). ERGs can have several positive effects on the organization, from identifying issues to enlightening coworkers to providing an opportunity for others to show support.
- Celebrate nationally recognized cultural days and months to acknowledge and foster respect for the myriad cultures that make up our society.

> "When people go to work, they shouldn't
> have to leave their hearts at home."
> —Betty Bender
> (Bender 2017)

STAGE 4: PEOPLE PROCESSES AUDITED

The DEIB strategy is supported by policies and systems that provide employees with a fair and safe environment to achieve their potential. The organization must regularly assess its people policies and systems for relevance to current internal and external climate factors and responsiveness to employee needs.

1. Audit policies and systems for bias and inequity. Look for explicit (conscious) bias, implicit (unconscious) bias, confirmation bias (information that matches preconceived beliefs). Conduct an audit of all policies that impact the employee experience to determine if they are fair, known, accessible, and used.

2. Ask employees how they feel about the systems and processes that affect them. Make them feel part of the process to have more equity and inclusion in the systems they have to use. Provide summary feedback on the findings to build trust.

3. Use the insights obtained in the audit and employee feedback to improve the systems and, ultimately, the employee experience. Benchmark against national or industry best practices to gauge the state of your people systems. Let employees know what changes you are contemplating and why. Don't miss the opportunity to acknowledge input and show that you listen.

[See Resource V for starter questions to assess your people processes.]

"Audit findings are easy to come up with, successful
change from a finding is the true internal audit value."
—Michael Piazza
(http://www.pda-usa.com/aw/features/quotes.php Michael piazza)

STAGE 5: RESULTS MEASURED

If you have come this far, you have made a significant investment in DEIB and should receive a return. While that return will ultimately be a greater diversity of thought throughout the organization, you should have goals and measurements along the way to show progress and success or identify problem areas to redress.

1. Set organizational DEIB goals to ensure everyone recognizes the importance of DEIB and the direction the organization is heading. Introduce departmental and individual goals as appropriate to drive accountability throughout the organization.
[See Resource III for sample organization DEIB goals and Resource IV for sample goals for individuals.]

2. Establish a regular cadence of communication for DEIB goals and initiatives to engage the team and get additional support and feedback. Utilize a variety of communication tools so that employees can access the information in the manner most comfortable for them. Regular communication will keep DEIB at the forefront of everyone's mind and provide momentum to pursue the goals.

3. Measuring and reporting on the results of activities supporting DEIB goals provides credibility to the mission. Measuring provides data and feedback that allow you to track progress and celebrate successes or change tactics as needed. Measurement of DEIB reinforces accountability for the organization and individuals. Measures should be

transparent and straightforward so the results can be easily understood and acted upon.

"On assessment: measure what you value instead
of valuing only what you can measure."
—Andy Hargreaves
(https://quotefancy.com/andy-hargreaves-quotes)

STAGE 6: SUSTAINING THE DIVERSITY, EQUITY, INCLUSION, AND BELONGING INITIATIVE

Once you've committed to making DEIB a core part of your culture and strategy, you need to nurture it to sustain the work.

Having a clear picture of what you expect from your DEIB effort is part of exploring "why" you want to do it; it is central to any communication, training, or measurement plans, and is the North Star for keeping it on track. This is a very conscious and intentional effort that should be considered in your initial DEIB strategy and modified to reflect internal or external changes to keep it relevant.

Some sustaining actions to consider include

- Designating a credible, interested, and willing leader (or leaders). If no one is given the responsibility and visibility of leading DEIB, it will be considered unimportant and participation optional. Establish a go-to person to champion the cause constantly;
- Being consistent in actions and words and modelling DEIB behaviors. Ensure that meetings, committees, and decision-making processes are diversely populated to encourage a wide range of ideas and opinions;
- Communicating DEIB goals and progress. Develop a regular communication cadence so that the organization recognizes its significance by keeping it in the forefront of their minds. Regular communication will also help normalize DEIB as a vital organization practice and strategy;

- Identifying and allocating DEIB resources like all other organization budgets or department planning processes. Establishing a budget to fund DEIB processes and activities eliminates the need for special requests that are often denied during business fluctuations. If this is important, plan for it;
- Ensuring employees have avenues to express concerns or opportunities. Formal processes that allow employees to convey their frustrations safely and without judgment and provide timely feedback will give management credibility and the DEIB initiative substance; and
- Evaluating the DEIB strategy and plan regularly, and changing as necessary. Like any other essential organization process, DEIB requires and deserves regular assessments and updates/corrections to stay aligned with the overall strategy and meet the needs of employees.

"A goal without a plan is just a wish."
—Antoine de Saint-Exupéry
(de Saint-Exupery 1943)

RESOURCES

I. DEIB CHANGE MANAGEMENT

DEIB is a significant culture change, and you should expect a wide array of individual responses to this initiative. A formal implementation process must be in place to ensure its success. There are many change management models, and your organization probably has one that it prefers. A robust change management process will address the Kübler-Ross Five-Stage Change Curve consisting of the following.

- Denial: "This can't be happening to me!"
- Anger: "This is wrong and I won't do it!"
- Bargaining: "What can I do to keep things as they are now?"
- Depression: "This is really bad. I don't think I can handle it."
- Acceptance: "This is not going away, so I guess I will give it a try. Maybe it will all work out."

The Kübler-Ross Change Curve

Combat the stages noted above by implementing a DEIB change management process that contains the following.

- Sponsorship: Ensure active support for the change at a senior executive level.
- Buy-in: Gain commitment for the changes from those involved and affected, directly or indirectly.
- Involvement: Involve the right people in designing and implementing changes to make sure they are sound.
- Impact: Assess and address how the changes will affect people.
- Communication: Convey who's affected by the changes.
- Readiness: Get people ready to adapt to the changes by ensuring they have the correct information, training, and help.

> "Change is hard because people overestimate the value of what they have—and underestimate the value of what they may gain by giving it up."
> —James Belasco and Ralph Stayer
> (James et al 1994)

II. COMMUNICATING DEIB

Managing the narrative on your DEIB initiative is necessary to avoid confusion, rumors, and disgruntlement due to negative perceptions and interpretations. The initial message needs to be honest, concise, and unequivocal. Getting the DEIB message to employees in a timely, consistent manner is imperative. Use all your communication channels to inform everyone: team meetings, email announcements, bulletin boards, newsletters, and so on. You only get one chance for a successful launch.

Outline for successful communication:

1) What is DEIB?
2) Why is this important now? Perspective of:
   i) Employees
   ii) Customers
   iii) Suppliers
   iv) Community
3) Leadership commitment and expectations
4) How does this impact me?
5) What changes will be seen?
6) When/Where/How will changes be initiated?
7) How will progress be monitored?
8) What resources are available?
9) How can I get involved?
10) When will we hear more?

Two sample DEIB initiative announcements follow.

SAMPLE COMMUNICATION 1

To: All Associates
Subject: Diversity, Equity, Inclusion, and Belonging

ORGANIZATION NAME is committed to valuing, developing, and respecting its people by providing them with opportunities to contribute and grow in a physically and emotionally safe work environment. As we strive to improve our organization, we have identified workplace diversity, equity, inclusion, and belonging (DEIB) as opportunities to positively impact our organization and workplace.

We should think of *diversity* as having a mix of people, experiences, and thoughts; *equity* as making sure everyone has a fair opportunity to succeed; and *inclusion* as appreciating and encouraging all to contribute their ideas and talents.

DEI impacts many aspects of our organization, including:

- Attracting and retaining the best talent in a competitive marketplace;
- Improving stakeholder perception since customers, suppliers, and our community places a high value on our commitment to DEI;
- Increasing innovation and overall performance; and
- Achieving a sustainable culture that attracts and values diverse talent, maintains (captures) institutional and job knowledge, and fosters an engaging and inclusive work environment will ensure the long-term viability of CLIENT NAME.

To address these challenges, we must have a culture that attracts, values, and retains the best talent in an engaging and inclusive work environment to ensure our success now and into the future. The best talent will come from many places and include many different types of people, and we must be able to demonstrate by our actions and our attitudes that these newcomers are welcome additions to the great team already in place.

In short order, you will be hearing about upcoming DEIB awareness courses, individual performance expectations, and opportunities to get involved in helping us foster a climate of diversity, equity, inclusion, and belonging in our organization.

Sincerely,

SAMPLE COMMUNICATION 2

To: All Associates
Re: Diversity, Equity, Inclusion, and Belonging

Our country is evolving demographically in ways that impact our markets, customers, competition, and our workforce. One out of two infants born today is a racial or ethnic minority member. In less than thirty years, our country will have a nonwhite majority. As the face of America changes, it makes sense that we change as well, which is why diversity, equity, inclusion, and belonging (DEIB) are a crucial part of our organizational strategy.

For us, diversity, equity, inclusion, and belonging includes the broadest possible range of backgrounds, experiences, cultures, and perspectives, all being equally valued, encouraged, and recognized for the contributions they bring to our thinking, problem-solving, and innovating. In addition to improving our organization, we believe this is the right thing to do.

Our quest for diversity, equity, inclusion, and belonging is not new, and we have seen some successes in the past. This is a commitment to do more, on an organization-wide scale, that is sustainable until it becomes embedded in our culture.

We are counting on you to embrace this initiative, participate in the training sessions and get involved in the volunteer groups and opportunities that will become available.

This is an exciting opportunity for our organization to develop a competitive advantage in our marketplace as we create a culture that values differences, offers fair treatment and opportunities, and encourages the participation and success of everyone.

Sincerely,

III. DEIB ORGANIZATIONAL GOAL SETTING

Goals make the vision actionable and allow for broad participation and support from the workforce.

Make sure your DEIB goals are SMART (specific, measurable, actionable, relevant, and timebound).

Commit to DEIB goals and plans in word and deed to set expectations and model desired behaviors.

Sample Goals

- Percentage of employees who respond to DEIB surveys
- Number of internal events/training with a target number of attendees
- Number or percentage of diverse candidates:
  - o in applicant pool
  - o interviewed
  - o hired
- Number of communications to employees on DEIB initiatives/ progress
- Number of job descriptions overhauled for inclusive language
- Number of processes evaluated for equity and unconscious bias
- Number or percentage of diverse suppliers
- Percentage increase in diverse representation in executive and management level roles
- Number or percentage of employees with DEIB goals

IV. DEIB INDIVIDUAL PERFORMANCE REVIEW GOAL SETTING

Awareness:

Goal: Enhance understanding of diversity and inclusion issues.
Goal met by: Viewing DEIB videos and discussing with manager/HR rep.

Goal: Participate in training that enhances my cultural competency.
Goal met by: Participating in LGBTQ awareness training during Pride Month.

Goal: Participate in professional activities that increase my experience interacting with people of cultural backgrounds different from my own.
Goal met by: Joining African American ERG to support activities and initiatives. Facilitating Hispanic focus group to address group issues and concerns.

Recruitment and Hiring:

Goal: Develop local/departmental recruiting plans to attract a diverse applicant pool for position vacancies.
Goal met by: Increasing diverse applicants by ___%. Identifying non-traditional recruiting sources to supply qualified diverse candidates.

Goal: Ensure recruiting/promotional materials and all on-site postings are culturally sensitive and accessible to all candidates and employees.

Goal met by: Establishing diverse team to review recruiting, promotional, and posted materials.

Goal: Provide position candidates with diverse interview panels to ensure different perspectives are presented and received during the process.

Goal met by: Identifying and training diverse interview panel candidates in practical and legal interview techniques. The panel meets to provide input into hiring decisions.

DEIB INDIVIDUAL PERFORMANCE REVIEW GOAL SETTING *(continued)*

Inclusion:

Goal: Create a safe environment by intentionally seeking participation from all team members in a respectful and nonjudgmental manner.
Goal met by: Quality of team meetings (improved participation). The quality and quantity of ideas/solutions reflect diverse inputs.

Goal: Promote diversity and inclusion on my team.
Goal met by: Encouraging development and advancement of underrepresented groups through coaching, training courses, and development opportunities.

Goal: Increase my knowledge and sensitivity to inclusion best practices.
Goal met by: Joining DEIB committees. Seeking and participating in online training courses through HR/training rep.

Equity:

Goal: Ensure policies are fairly implemented in my area by regularly reviewing the progress of underrepresented groups to identify opportunities for intervention and support.
Goal met by: Achieving (or improving) pay, promotion, and development standings for target groups relative to the majority group experience.

Goal: Provide coaching and mentoring resources to my employees as desired or needed for continued engagement and development.
Goal met by: Assigning coaches/mentors, and providing time for meaningful interactions. Target employees provide feedback on the success of the exchanges.

V. REVIEW PROCESSES FOR DEIB BIAS

Ensuring that your policies and procedures support your DEIB initiative is critical. Failure to align your internal practices with your stated DEIB objectives will cause a lack of credibility and buy-in to the cause. Use an audit procedure to assess processes for their DEIB strengths and weaknesses. Here are a few questions to get you started:

- Recruiting (Diversity):

  o Do job descriptions and postings contain discriminatory language?
  o Do recruiting sources reach diverse candidates?
  o Does your employer brand emphasize diversity?

- Selection (Inclusion):

  o Do selection pools intentionally contain diverse candidates?
  o Are interviewers trained to value diverse experiences?
  o Are selection criteria based on objective position requirements and not biased preferences?

- Onboarding (Belonging):

  o Is DEIB a discussion topic in the onboarding session?
  o Is the team prepared to welcome each new employee?
  o Do you provide time for settling in and following up?

- Performance management (Equity):

  o Is performance feedback based on objective criteria?
  o Are desired DEIB behaviors recognized in performance reviews?
  o Does your data suggest favoritism to one group over others?

- Training and development (Diversity and Inclusion):

  o Are training opportunities announced and made available to all employees?
  o Do management/leadership development programs include diverse participants?
  o Do training programs encourage diversity of thought?

- Succession planning (Diversity, Inclusion, Belonging):

  o Does success plan data suggest favoritism due to a lack of diversity?
  o Are succession plan criteria free of bias?
  o Does the succession plan talent pool include non-traditional candidates?

- Compensation (Equity):

  o Does the data show a pay disparity between genders, races, or other criteria?
  o Are compensation practices transparent to employees?
  o Are managers trained and monitored in administering bias-free compensation programs?

Note that while employees judge an organization's DEIB culture based on established processes such as these, the observable management actions and attitudes are the true barometer of an organization's sincerity and commitment to DEIB.

CONCLUSION

You are immensely talented and capable. So are the people around you in your work and social relationships. Be humble enough to recognize that you don't have all the answers and hungry enough to want them.

Value the unique backgrounds and experiences of the people in your orbit. Encourage the sharing of different perspectives so that you and your organization can consider a broad range of possibilities and solutions.

The goal is to create an environment that consistently generates diverse thoughts and that can be used or combined to create a better outcome and advantage. Embracing diversity, equity, inclusion, and belonging are the keys to creating this environment. When people are informed and feel needed and appreciated, they will contribute their thoughts and energies to your cause if you allow them to. They will also develop a sense of ownership for the outcome and a willingness to try new approaches to situations.

Not every idea will be helpful for the challenge at hand, and many can be respectfully dismissed or set aside for future consideration. Wayne Gretzky said, "you miss one hundred percent of the shots you don't take." Similarly, you miss every idea or suggestion you don't allow to be expressed. Invite people who see things differently to help you and your organization develop the best solutions for your stakeholders. This is thoughtful diversity.

REFERENCES

Belasco, James A. and Ralph C. Stayer. 1993. *Flight of the Buffalo.* New York: Grand Central Publishing

Bender, Betty. 2017. https://digitalbusinessblog.wordpress.com/2017/05/15/when-people-go-to-work-they-shouldn't-have-to-leave-their-hearts-at-home-betty-bender/

Bersin, Josh. 2019. "Why Diversity and Inclusion Has Become a Business Priority." Josh Bersin. https://joshbersin.com/2015/12/why-diversity-and-inclusion-will-be-a-top-priority-for-2016/.

Bourke, Juliet, and Bernadette Dillon. 2018. "The diversity and inclusion revolution: eight powerful truths." *Deloitte Review* 22 (January): 81–95. https://www2.deloitte.com/content/dam/insights/us/articles/4209 Diversity-and-inclusion-revolution/DI Diversity-and-inclusion-revolution.pdf.

Brown, Brené. 2017. *Braving the Wilderness: The Quest for True Belonging and the Courage to Stand Alone.* New York: Random House.

Browning, Robert. 1855. *Andrea del Sarto.* Poetry Foundation. https://www.poetryfoundation.org/poems/43745/andrea-del-sarto.

Cho, Janet H. 2016. "'Diversity is being invited to the party; inclusion is being asked to dance,' Verna Myers tells Cleveland Bar." Cleveland.com. https://www.cleveland.com/business/2016/05/diversity is being invited to.html.

Covey, Stephen R. 1989. *The Seven Habits of Highly Effective People.* New York: Fireside.

de Pree, Max. 2004. *Leadership is an Art.* New York: Random House.

de Saint-Exupery, Antoine. 1943. *Le Petit Prince.* New York: Reynal and Hitchcock

Gebreyes, Micah. n.d. "5 Benefits of diversity and inclusion in the workplace." Greenhouse. https://www.greenhouse.io/blog/5-benefits-of-diversity-in-the-workplace#:~:text=Literally%20 bring%20in%20the%20cash,that%20can't%20be%20ignored.

Glassdoor. 2021. "What Job Seekers Really Think About Your Diversity and Inclusion Stats." Glassdoor. https://www.glassdoor.com/employers/blog/diversity/.

Hunt, Vivian, Dennis Layton, and Sara Prince. 2015. "Why Diversity Matters." McKinsey & Company. https://www.mckinsey.com/business-functions/people-and-organizational-performance/our-insights/why-diversity-matters.

Jakes, TD. 2016. (https://facebook.com/bishopjakes/posts/if-you-dont-have-commitment-you- cannot-bring-down-the-giants-in-any-area-of-your/10154459820918322)

Kurtz, Annalynn, and Tal Yellin. n.d. "Millennial generation is bigger, more diverse than boomers." CNN Business. https://money.cnn.com/interactive/economy/diversity-millennials-boomers/index.html.

Larson, Erik. 2017. "Research Shows Diversity + Inclusion = Better Decision Making at Work." Cloverpop. https://www.cloverpop.com/blog/research-shows-diversity-inclusion-better-decision-making-at-work.

Lorenzo, Rocío, Nicole Voigt, Miki Tsusaka, Matt Krentz, and Katie Abouzahr. 2018. "How Diverse Leadership Teams Boost Innovation." BCG. https://www.bcg.com/publications/2018/how-diverse-leadership-teams-boost-innovation.

Moran, Gwen. 2017. "How These Top Companies Are Getting Inclusion Right." Fast Company. https://www.fastcompany.com/3067346/how-these-top-companies-are-getting-inclusion-right.

Riordan, Rick. 2011. *The Red Pyramid*. New York: Hyperion.

United Nations Office for the Coordination of Humanitarian Affairs. 2019. "Gender equality is not only a women's issue—it is everyone's issue." UNOCHA.org. https://www.unocha.org/story/%E2%80%9Cgender-equality-not-only-

women%E2%80%99s-issue-it-everyone%E2%80%99s-
issue%E2%80%9D#:~:text=%E2%80%9CGender%20
equality%20is%20not%20only%20a%20women's%20issue%20
%E2%80%93%20it's%20everyone's,a%20better%2Dbalanced%20
world.%E2%80%9D.

Printed in the United States
by Baker & Taylor Publisher Services